Make Your Own Vineyard

Ex Vite Vita

Dr. ANDREA SCARSI

Copyright © 2015 Andrea Scarsi

All rights reserved.

ISBN-10: 1542436699
ISBN-13: 978-1542436694

DEDICATED

To my Father, son of a wine land, who always wanted to drink with me, while I preferred other delicacies.

It was just after his death, finding myself inheriting hundreds of bottles, and feeling that I had to drink them all in his memory and honor, which I quickly did, that I got into the cheerfulness of wine and new dedicated friends, first Mr. Gian Antonio Posocco (Nalin), master of Assiria Natural Wines, who also led me into the endless domain of exotic smells, tastes, and companionship.

TABLE OF CONTENTS

	Note of the Author	i
1	Presentation	Pg 1
2	Introduction	Pg 2
3	Why Start A Vineyard	Pg 3
4	Essential Points About Grape Growing	Pg 5
5	Selecting Viable Land For A Vineyard	Pg 7
6	In Focus: Ideal Soil For Grape Vines	Pg 9
7	Vineyard Preparation	Pg 11
8	Notes On Using Organic Fertilizers	Pg 13
9	Naturally-Available Nutrients In Manure	Pg 15
10	Guidelines For Limestone & Nutrients Application	Pg 16
11	Preparing The Vineyard For The Planting Season	Pg 19
12	Planting Cover Crops In The Vineyard	Pg 21
13	Designing Your Vineyard	Pg 23
14	General Guidelines For Vineyard Design	Pg 24
15	Proper Row Positioning	Pg 25
16	General Layout Of The Vineyard	Pg 30
17	Step By Step Guide To Installing A Trellis System	Pg 31
18	Checklist For The Annual Care Of Grape Vineyards	Pg 34

19	Guidelines For Selecting Grape Cultivars	Pg 46
20	Grape Species & Cultivars	Pg 51
21	Planting The Grapes	Pg 55
22	Organic Farming & Disease Management	Pg 60
23	Summing Up	Pg 62
24	Appendix 1 2 3 4 5 6	Pg 71
25	About the Author	Pg 83
26	Books by Andrea Scarsi	Pg 85
27	Mantras by Andrea Scarsi	Pg 86
28	Books by Andrea Scarsi in Italian	Pg 87

NOTE OF THE AUTHOR

The Author has strived to be as accurate and complete as possible in the creation of this report, notwithstanding the fact that he does not warrant or represent at any time that the contents within are absolute and unequivocal due to the rapidly changing nature of the collective consciousness and Internet.

While all attempts have been made to verify the information provided in this publication, the Author assumes no responsibility for errors, omissions, or contrary interpretation of the subject matter herein.

Any perceived slights of specific persons, peoples, companies, or organizations are genuinely unintentional.

In practical advice books and manuals, just like anything else in life, there are no guarantees of results being performed, or income made, as one expects. Readers are cautioned to rely on their own judgment about their individual circumstances and act accordingly.

This book is not intended for use as a source of legal, business, accounting, medical, psychological, or financial advice. Readers are advised to seek services of competent professionals in all the aforementioned fields.

Enjoy.

www.andrea-scarsi.com

PRESENTATION

Making your own vineyard is easy, if you really want to; you've just got to know how, where, and when, and that's it. Now, you can happily gather every bit of information from the comfort of your own home, in just a few days, and having fun. *Make Your Own Vineyard* is a practical manual for you, if you're interested in learning everything there is to know about grape growing.

It tells you how to start a vineyard, plant it properly, placing the rows, installing a trellis system, caring throughout the year, selecting the cultivars, when to seek professional help, pruning, buying essential supplies, watering, protecting from pests, and more. Yes, having plump, juicy grapes, it's truly possible; you just need to know how.

Follow the instructions and enjoy.

Cheers!

INTRODUCTION

Nowadays, it is completely possible to start your very own vineyard to grow grapes. There are essentially two types of lands or areas used to grow grapes: traditional areas and non-traditional areas. It is fortunate that many backyard grape growers have had much success in establishing grape vineyards in non-traditional areas.

Even climate and soil quality are no longer problems to the backyard grape grower, as long as specific guidelines are followed when tending to the vineyard and growing the grapes. This book will become your essential guide to achieving all your goals in starting and maintaining your very own personal vineyard.

If you are looking for the perfect area for a new vineyard, always remember that grape vines require easy access to direct sunlight if they are to bloom and grow adequately. The first three years of the vineyard will be essential to the health of all the grape cultivars that you will be planting in the vineyard. Opt for wide open land areas with few structures and tall trees.

While it is possible to coax grape cultivars to grow in poorly ventilated areas, fungi problems are common when there isn't enough air circulating among the vines. Lack of adequate direct sunlight is also a contributing factor to many problems in the vineyard.

WHY START A VINEYARD?

There are several good reasons to start a grape vineyard of your own:

1. Many entrepreneurs are exploring the possibility of grape production, so you won't be alone when you finally start your own vineyard.

2. Wine production facilities have been established continually throughout many states in the US, but grape production has fallen behind.

Simply put: the market needs more grapes. And if you start your own vineyard and succeed in planting and growing grapes, you are immediately tapping into a market that will not be drying up (perhaps forever - since wine making has been around since the earliest era of Western civilization!).

3. There is a consistently high demand for quality grapes that can be used as raw material for regional wines (such as Cabernets).

4. Having a vineyard means you can enjoy the sunlight and work the earth to produce top class, tasty grapes.

5. Planting grapes is a good idea if you have an existing area of land that is not fit to grow other types of common agricultural crops. Again, there is a ready market for your produce, so you won't have to worry about losing any of your investments in this endeavor.

Important Note: Like other agricultural undertakings, starting your own vineyard will require you to invest a significant amount of capital upfront. Exploring your financing options is a logical first step in the process of acquiring viable land for the up-and-coming vineyard.

ESSENTIAL POINTS ABOUT GRAPE GROWING

Here are some essential points to consider before embarking on grape growing:

1. To be a successful grape grower, you must be involved in all aspects of the cultivation process, from vineyard maintenance to the post-harvest phase.

2. A working knowledge of plant culture would be an excellent addition to your tools when you are starting out with your vineyard.

3. In addition to working the land alongside your employees (if you wish to hire some workers), you have to be keen on marketing as well. The business end of this endeavor will ensure that you will be amply rewarded for your efforts at the vineyard.

4. Thinking of purchasing an existing vineyard? You may encounter some difficulties as the general scarcity of vineyards have resulted in steep prices. Vineyard owners are also unwilling to sell their land because of the high demand for their produce, year after year.

Grape vineyards have several markets to cater to: fresh grapes, frozen grapes, grape concentrate, grape juice, and wine.

Among these five markets, many agree that producing excellent grapes for wineries is the most profitable option - and perhaps the wisest option, based on the market trends and demands of the present time.

Of course, each state will have its own peculiarities when it comes to the demand for grapes and grape products, so it's up to you to discover just what your region or locality needs at the moment.

This is one of the great things when you own a vineyard - you can become a flexible producer and you can respond fairly well to shifts or changes in the market demand.

Are you interested in producing fresh table grapes, seedless or otherwise? There is a small, yet sustainable market for fresh grapes.

However, it has been judged that the production cost and other production requirements of table grapes is higher than those needed for wine grapes. It's up to you what particular market you wish to respond to when you're drafting a solid business plan for your vineyard.

On the other hand, vineyards that produce wine grapes can opt to associate or market directly with one or several wineries. This ensures that every harvest is bought directly by bulk and the chances of having unsold batches of grapes is greatly reduced.

Processing (such as pressing of the grapes to produce grape juice or concentrates) is also an option that you can explore to expand your market reach. For example, with grape concentrate you have two markets - wineries and juice manufacturers.

SELECTING VIABLE LAND FOR A VINEYARD

The formula for success in the grape-growing business is fairly simple: you need to consistently produce high quality grapes either for processing or direct consumption and you have to grow highly marketable cultivars or grape varieties.

As with other agricultural crops, hybrid varieties of grapes abound. Each hybrid was made to fit a particular region or zone - we will touch upon these hybrids later on. For now, let's look at the steps needed to select viable land for a grape vineyard.

There are no hard and fast rules when it comes to selecting a good site. There are, however, general guidelines that you can follow to make the selection easier:

1. Grape vineyards require adequate soil drainage.

2. Winter temperatures in the region or locality should be at a moderate range (extreme winter temperatures can result in large losses, as you will see when you are performing post-winter pruning and general vineyard maintenance).

Are grapes sensitive to extreme cold and winters? Yes. Frost injuries are common in very cold zones in the US. If this happens to your vineyard, early breakage of the young grape buds is almost imminent.

3. There should be excellent air circulation in the area to minimize fungi-related crop problems.

4. Extremes in temperature and constant fluctuations in the

environmental temperature can predispose grape vines to disease.

5. Grape vines produce more grapes if the root system of the plants are well developed. For this to become possible, the soil must be partly-loose and rich in organic matter.

The looseness of the earth will allow even the slimmest components of the root system to anchor firmly into the soil. Large amounts of organic matter in the soil will contribute greatly to the continuous growth of the grape vines.

IN FOCUS: IDEAL SOIL FOR GRAPE VINES

Soil examination is the next logical step during site selection. The soil must be able to provide good anchorage and aeration to the grape vines.

Are grape cultivars picky with the soil? Not necessarily. However, if your goal is to have an abundant yield of marketable grapes, year after year, then it is absolutely essential that you comes as close as possible to ideal, grape-growing conditions.

The following are the characteristics of viable soil fit for growing grapes:

1. Soils with moderate fertility are adequate for growing grapes.

2. Internal drainage and surface drainage must be efficient. The soil's drainage is actually the most important factor of grape growing. If the drainage is not taken care of properly, the grapes will not be able to grow correctly.

3. The depth of usable soil must be thirty to forty inches (at least) before denser soil layers are reached.

4. Ideal soil is partly sandy and partly loamy. ("Loamy" means lots of natural organic matter.)

Important Note: When the soil's drainage is consistently poor, the root system of the grapes will not be able to spread out as deeply as possible into the soil substrate. Soils with poor drainage probably have high water tables and impenetrable lower layers.

If you plant grapes on such soil, two things can probably happen: the grape yield will be low and the vines will not survive for more than a few years. In good soil, grapes can grow for several years, provided that the proper pruning and maintenance is given.

Ideal chemical properties of vineyard soil are:
1. Soil pH level - 5.5 to 6.8
2. Organic matter content - 3%
3. Phosphorous level - 50 pounds/acre
4. Potassium level - up to 300 pounds/acre
5. Magnesium content - up to 250 pounds/acre
6. Zinc content - up to 10 pounds/acre
7. Boron content - 2 pounds/acre

VINEYARD PREPARATION

If the soil's pH level is too acidic, ground limestone can be applied to the acidic soil to reach a more desirable pH level (neutral to slightly alkaline soil is good for grape growing).

Additional nutrients and fertilizers like phosphorous should be added to the soil only after the careful measurement of the soil's chemical properties.

For example, if the phosphorous level of the soil is already at the 300 pounds/acre level, the addition of phosphorous should be reduced.

Inversely, lands with low mineral levels detected during soil sampling will require additional fertilizers and minerals before planting to bring the nutrient level up to a more acceptable range.

According to guidelines from the USDA, if the soil in question has been proven to have 1,600 pounds/acre or more of phosphorous, no additional phosphorous should be added to the soil for any reason.

Careful consideration should also be given to land areas that are in close proximity to natural bodies of water such as streams and rivers, because agricultural runoff can affect the quality of the water and may produce long-term problems for the soil and the natural waterway.

Consult with your local state board for agriculture before

adding fertilizers and other chemicals to your land and follow the state board's guidelines.

If you already have viable land for a new vineyard, you can take a representative sample of the land's soil to an agricultural laboratory or experimental station for analysis.

A core sample can be obtained by digging up to seven inches into the soil. For non-traditional vineyard areas like lawns, you can reduce the depth to about four inches. It is recommended that vineyard owners perform a soil analysis of their land every two years.

NOTES ON USING ORGANIC FERTILIZERS

Many vineyard owners prefer applying organic manure and tobacco stalks to naturally fertilize their land. To help you decide which type of organic fertilizer is a good choice for your land (based on soil tests), here is a breakdown of the nutrient content of the most common manures.

Dairy cattle: Water Content 80%, Nitrogen Content 11 pounds/ton, Phosphorous Content 9 pounds/ton, Potassium Content 12 pounds/ton.

Swine: Water Content 80%, Nitrogen Content 9 pounds/ton, Phosphorous Content 9 pounds/ton, Potassium Content 11 pounds/ton.

Beef cattle: Water Content 80%, Nitrogen Content 11 pounds/ton, Phosphorous Content 7 pounds/ton, Potassium Content 10 pounds/ton.

Broiler litter: Water Content 20%, Nitrogen Content 55 pounds/ton, Phosphorous Content 55 pounds/ton, Potassium Content 45 pounds/ton.

Broiler layer: Water Content 40%, Nitrogen Content 35 pounds/ton, Phosphorous Content 55 pounds/ton, Potassium Content 30 pounds/ton.

Broiler pullets: Water Content 30%, Nitrogen Content 40 pounds/ton, Phosphorous Content 45 pounds/ton, Potassium Content 40 pounds/ton.

Goat: Water Content 70%, Nitrogen Content 22 pounds/ton, Phosphorous Content 5 pounds/ton, Potassium Content 15 pounds/ton.

Horse: Water Content 80%, Nitrogen Content 12 pounds/ton, Phosphorous Content 6 pounds/ton, Potassium Content 12 pounds/ton.

Tobacco stalks: Water Content 20%, Nitrogen Content 30 pounds/ton, Phosphorous Content 10 pounds/ton, Potassium Content 70 pounds/ton.

While it is true that organic manure is touted as an exceptional alternative to commercial fertilizers, it should be noted that the availability of the nutrients varies from one year to another.

For example, if organic potash is applied this year, only eighty percent of the total potassium content of the soil will be available the next year.

The availability of usable nitrogen content of the manure in question is dependent on several factors:

1. Livestock diet
2. Species of the livestock
3. Storage method
4. Handling method
5. Schedule of manure application (time of the year)
6. How the manure is applied to the soil

Despite the quirks of using organic manure to add nutrients to the vineyard soil, organic manure is actually a rich source of various other nutrients that can contribute to the fertility of the soil for the long term.

NATURALLY-AVAILABLE NUTRIENTS IN MANURE

Among these available nutrients in manure are:
1. Molybdenum
2. Copper
3. Magnesium
4. Sulfuric compounds
5. Zinc
6. Calcium

Since organic manure is rich in nutrients, it is highly recommended for vineyard properties that have been evaluated as having very low organic content (less than 2% organic matter) after soil sampling.

If you wish to naturally condition the soil before planting begins, another option is tobacco stalks. Cut tobacco stalks collected after the harvest must be covered to prevent the loss of the nutrients due to rainfall. The process of nutrient loss through natural means is called leaching and should be avoided at all cost if tobacco stalks are to be used.

GUIDELINES FOR LIMESTONE & NUTRIENTS APPLICATION

The adjustment of the reserved acidity of the soil should be made at least 3 months before the planting of the grapes formally commences. Based on research, the following ideal pH ranges for grapes have been established:

1.) American hybrids - 6.5 during planting, 5.5 to 6.0 during production phase.

2.) French-American hybrids - 6.5 during planting, up to 6.0 during production phase.

3.) European grapes - no less than 6.0 during establishment, up to 7.0 during production phase.

If nitrogen application has been deemed necessary after examination of a core sample of the soil, do not apply more than one hundred pounds of nitrogen for every acre of your vineyard.

Roughly, that's just 3.7 ounces of nitrogen for every one hundred square feet of land. Nitrogen application must be timed well, too: the application of this nutrient is most needed during the planting season.

Grapes, blueberries and other similar fruit-bearing crops require lots of magnesium to produce a significant yield. If the soil's magnesium level is below 120 pounds per acre, then additional magnesium has to be added.

These guidelines are applicable only during the planting season or the establishment phase. After establishment, soil examination and plant culture must be made to ascertain what other nutrients must be added to the soil to boost grape production.

The following tables are application guides for potassium, magnesium and phosphate fertilizers.

Amount of Phosphate in the Soil:
Amount of Phosphate Needed During Establishment
70 pounds/acre or more: No additional phosphate is needed.
35 to less than 70 pounds/acre: Up to 80 pounds/acre or up to 3 ounces/100 square feet
Less than 35 pounds/acre: 80 to 120 pounds/acre or 3 to 5 ounce/100 square feet

Amount of Potassium in the Soil:
Amount of Potassium Needed During Establishment
300 pounds/acre: No additional potassium is needed
200 pounds/acre but less than 300 pounds/acre: 80 pounds/acre or 3 ounces/100 square feet
Less than 200 pounds/acre: 80 to 120 pounds/acre or 3 to 5 ounces/100 square feet

Amount of Magnesium in the Soil:
Amount of Magnesium Needed During Establishment
Below 60 pounds/acre: 80 pounds/acre
61 to 120 pounds/acre: 20 to 80 pounds/acre
120 pounds/acre or more: No additional magnesium is needed

This following table shows how much ground limestone is needed (in tons/acre) to attain a pH level of 6.4 after soil sampling has yielded the present pH level of the soil:

Water pH Level=Buffer pH of 5.5>5.7>5.9>6.1>6.3>6.5>6.7>6.9
4.5=4.50>4.25>4.00>3.50>3.00>2.50>2.00>1.50
4.7=4.50>4.25>4.00>3.50>3.00>2.50>2.00>1.50
4.9=4.50>4.25>3.75>3.25>2.75>2.25>1.75>1.25
5.1=4.50>4.25>3.75>3.25>2.75>2.25>1.75>1.25
5.3=4.50>4.25>3.75>3.25>2.50>2.00>1.50>1.00
5.5=4.50>4.25>3.50>3.00>2.50>2.00>1.50>1.00
5.7=4.50>4.00>3.50>2.75>2.25>1.75>1.25>1.00
5.9=0.00>4.00>3.25>2.50>2.00>1.50>1.00>0.75
6.1=0.00>0.00>2.75>2.00>1.50>0.75>0.50>1.00

If you wish to raise the soil's pH level to 6.6:
Water pH Level=Buffer pH of 5.5>5.7>5.9>6.1>6.3>6.5>6.7>6.9
4.5=4.50>4.50>4.00>3.75>3.25>2.75>2.25>1.50
4.7=4.50>4.50>4.00>3.75>3.25>2.50>2.00>1.50
4.9=4.50>4.50>4.00>3.75>3.00>2.50>2.00>1.50
5.1=4.50>4.50>4.00>3.50>3.00>2.50>2.00>1.50
5.3=4.25>4.50>4.00>3.50>3.00>2.50>1.75>1.25
5.5=4.25>4.50>4.00>3.50>2.75>2.25>1.75>1.25
5.7=4.50>4.50>4.00>3.25>2.75>2.25>1.50>1.25
5.9=0.00>4.50>4.00>3.25>2.50>2.00>1.50>1.00
6.1=0.00>0.00>3.75>3.00>2.25>1.75>1.25>0.75
6.3=0.00>0.00>0.00>2.50>1.75>1.20>0.75>0.50

To raise the soil's pH level to the 6.8 range:
Water pH Level=Buffer pH of 5.5>5.7>5.9>6.1>6.3>6.5>6.7>6.9
4.5=4.20>4.50>4.25>4.00>3.50>2.75>2.25>1.75
4.7=4.25>4.50>4.25>4.00>3.50>2.75>2.25>1.75
4.9=4.25>4.50>4.25>3.75>3.25>2.75>2.25>1.75
5.1=4.50>4.50>4.25>3.75>3.25>2.75>2.25>1.50
5.3=4.75>4.50>4.25>3.75>3.25>2.75>2.00>1.50
5.5=5.00>4.50>4.25>3.75>3.25>2.50>2.00>1.50
5.7=5.50>4.50>4.25>3.75>3.25>2.50>2.00>1.50
5.9=0.00>4.25>4.25>3.75>3.00>2.50>1.75>1.25
6.1=0.00>0.00>4.50>3.75>3.00>2.25>1.75>1.25
6.3=0.00>0.00>0.00>3.50>2.75>2.00>1.50>1.00
6.5=0.00>0.00>0.00>0.00>2.25>1.50>1.00>0.75

PREPARING THE VINEYARD FOR THE PLANTING SEASON

Vineyard preparation prior to actual grape planting involves three major phases:

1. Plowing - Plowing is done to open up the soil and 'turn it over', bringing the drier upper layer closer to the moist subsoil and vice versa. Plowing also improves the aeration of the soil and prepares it for planting.

2. Sub-soiling - Sub-soiling is performed to break apart the pan layer of the plowed land.

3. Leveling - Leveling is the final step of preparing the vineyard. The soil is leveled with tractors and is now ready for planting (given that the soil's pH level and nutrient content has already been adjusted).

Newly prepared vineyards should also be free from the various perennial weeds that are considered pests to grapes.

Some known weed pests include:
Thistle
Johnsongrass
Quackgrass
Dock
Brambles
Black medic

Broadleaf plantain
Common purslane
Dandelion
Ground ivy
Crabgrass
Mouse-eared chickweed
Prostrate knotweed
Speedwell
White clover
Wild onions
Wild garlic
Yellow wood sorrel

Many weed pests found in wide open farmlands can survive for years, regardless of inclement weather and change of seasons. Weeds survive by going dormant and by becoming propagules.

Examples of propagules are:
Below-ground rhizomes
Tubers
Budding rootstocks
Budding tap-roots
Above-ground stolons

Perennial weed pests are much harder to control because the propagules are usually protected by the soil and organic debris usually found in vineyards. Annual weed pests are much easier to deal with.

It is recommended that if perennial weed pests do exist in your land, that you deal with weed pests by using herbicides. Note that many herbicides that are indicated for controlling perennial weed pests can only be safely used during the establishment phase and not during the production and harvesting phases.

PLANTING COVER CROPS IN THE VINEYEARD

Cover crops are needed in vineyards to prevent extreme soil erosion. These plants also provide an easy source of extra nutrients throughout the year.

In addition to protecting the integrity and nutrient content of the soil, cover crops are also used to reduce the growth and propagation of weed pests and animal pests in the vineyard.

Temporary Cover Crops

Here are some steps to establish a temporary cover crop before the permanent cover crop is planted in the vineyard:

1. Apply lime to raise or lower the pH level of the soil, as needed.

2. After testing the soil, add nutrients to the soil (again, as needed).

3. Plant a cover crop like Sudan grass over the newly plowed earth. Cover crops like the Sudan grass can be planted successfully until the month of August.

Permanent Cover Crop

When it's time to grow permanent crop cover in the vineyard, the soil is plowed once again (under the temporary cover crop) before the permanent cover crop is planted.

In the Midwest, establishment of cover crop is usually done

from early August to the middle of September.

Fescue and perennial rye can be planted as permanent cover crops - eighty to one hundred twenty pounds per acre would be sufficient to cover the entire floor of a new vineyard adequately.

Drop-seeding is used to cover the entire vineyard with cover crop seeds (this can be done up to late summer). The cover crop will attain full maturity in spring of the next year.

The final stage of vineyard preparation can be done in summer (usually it starts in March).

Soil cultivation is much easier during the hottest months of the year because the soil is dry enough and loose enough for plowing and leveling. Fourteen days before the grape vines are to be planted, rows of cover crop are permanently killed with the application of a systemic herbicide.

These areas where weed pests and cover crops are removed are called "killed rows". This is where the vines should be planted. "Killed rows" are usually situated in between cover crop rows and supported by posts. Before planting can commence, the dry ground cover must be destroyed through tilling to allow the grape vines to be planted.

DESIGNING YOUR VINEYEARD

If you are ready to design your vineyard, it is assumed that you have completed the following:
Soil sampling
Adjustment of soil pH level
Adding necessary nutrients to the soil
First tilling
Sub-soiling
Leveling

These should be your specific goals when designing a vineyard:

1. Maximize the bearing capacity of the land per acre and with the least amount of time.

2. Optimize the production of grape vines.

3. Reduce or prevent destructive erosion of the soil.

4. Increase the efficiency at which vine management is carried out.

5. Facilitate the use of farming equipment and vehicles throughout the whole vineyard.

GENERAL GUIDELINES FOR VINEYEARD DESIGN

A main plan of the entire vineyard has to be drawn up prior to the actual implementation of any changes to the land. You should be able to see nearby roads, existing rows of land, and points in the entire land where tool sheds and storage structures are situated.

If you have a large piece of land, the entire area of the property should be divided into more manageable 'blocks' of land. This can be done through professional surveying (a geodetic engineer can help).

All sides of the vineyard should have accessible space equal to the space in between killed rows and cover crops.

If your property is large, usable blocks of land should be separated by wider avenues to facilitate air circulation. Poor air circulation can result in many problems during the production phase of your vineyard.

PROPER ROW POSITIONING

There are several factors that affect the proper direction and placement of rows:
1. Amount of light available and the direction of the light
2. Slope (steepness) of the vineyard
3. Consistent wind speeds in the area

Usually, rows that run from the north to south are able to get more sunlight than rows that run from east to the west.

If you think the natural shade of nearby trees could be a problem, you should design your rows to run from the north to the south and the rows should be spaced closely together

In this type of situation, the wider the separation of the rows, the less sunlight the rows receive.

If the area is generally windy, the direction of the killed rows should be parallel to the direction of the strong winds and not perpendicular or against the wind (doing so will damage your vines and reduce production).

If you plan on establishing a raisin vineyard, then the rows should run from east to west (as opposed to north to south). The rows in between the grape vines will receive extra light, which is important when drying grapes.

Should the spacing between the rows be based entirely on the size of the farming equipment you have? No. In fact, newly established vineyards should have ideal row spacing to encourage maximum growth of the grape vines.

The equipment used on the vineyard should conform to the existing ideal spacing and not the other way around. A well-spaced vineyard will outlast farm equipment by years because the land will continually give life to hard-wearing and very productive grape vines.

NOTES ON PROPER ROW SPACING

Proper row spacing allows the vineyard owner to install proper trellising systems for the grape vines. Many vineyards have rows that are nine to ten feet away from each other, while some go as far as twelve feet for every row.

Larger gaps between rows may be needed to accommodate changes in the slope of the land. The use of training techniques such as the Geneva Double Curtain also necessitates wider spacing between the rows of grape vines.

Is row spacing important? It is very important because it directly affects the yield or production rate of the vineyard. The principle behind row spacing is quite clear: the wider the spaces between the actual rows of grape vines, the less the produce of the vineyard per acre.

What particular factors are used to determine proper row spacing? Two factors stand out from all the rest:

1.) The productive rigor of the grape cultivar.
2.) The expected size of the vines at maturity.

The spacing of the vines themselves in each row also has a bearing on the productivity of the vineyard. The closer each vine is to each other, the more productive each row - but only for a short period of time.

Once the vines reach a particular size, the shade produced begins to reduce the amount of available sunlight to the grape vines.

This eventually reduces the productive yield of the vines. This is the reason why in the long-term, adequate spacing between each vine is recommended.

Every foot of grape vine can easily support up to eight grape buds.

However, it has been shown that vines which are allowed to grow more than six buds per foot are less resistant to winter problems. In addition to possible winter problems, it has also been reported that grapes produced from such vines have lower juice quality.

If juice quality is affected, the marketability of your grapes (and other processed products from your vineyard) might go down, because wineries generally require top quality juice.

If you are using an American hybrid grape cultivar or an American-French grape cultivar, you may want to consider planting the vines eight feet apart from each other.

This technique has proven to be very satisfactory in terms of producing quality yields over the years. (However, average climate conditions and soil quality are required.)

For European grape cultivars, planting an average of seven vines is recommended.

How many grape vines does one need to get a significantly good yield of grapes during harvest? Based on statistics, you would need at least six hundred individual grape vines or more for every acre of land that you have.

For single canopy systems, the spacing for American hybrid cultivars and French-American hybrid cultivars is eight feet by nine feet, which is roughly equivalent to 605 individual vines per acre.

For European cultivars that are maintained through a similar training system, the recommended spacing is seven feet by eight feet, which is equivalent to 778 vines per acre - this number is enough to produce a very significant yield per harvest, if average conditions in the vineyard are maintained.

In time, the spacing between the vines can be increased to

ten feet. This is done to reduce establishment costs in the future.

However, large spacing between individual vines translates to higher operating costs because the air pressure needed to deliver pesticides will have to be increased to adequately cover each plant in the vineyard.

GENERAL LAYOUT OF THE VINEYEARD

Should you use a square layout or a rectangular layout? Vineyard owners state that you can save a lot of time (and money) if you lay out your rows in a rectangular layout, rather than a square layout.

There are two main advantages to using a rectangular layout:

1. A rectangular layout allows more vines to be planted per acre of land. Hence, you have a bigger harvest.

2. A rectangular layout also means that you have longer rows. Tractors and other similar farm vehicles don't have to turn too many times during regular maintenances, as opposed to a strictly square vineyard layout.

If you want to use a rectangular layout, know that heavy soils can support load-bearing rows of up to 700 feet in length. If you wish to use drip irrigation, a row can be as long as 600 feet.

Vineyards that have been installed with a sprinkler irrigation system, as opposed to a drip irrigation system, can have rows as long as 1,000 feet each.

However, then each weight-bearing row must have strong head assemblies to be able to sustain such a weight. In drier areas in the United States, drip irrigation is recommended to reduce the incidence of plant diseases.

STEP BY STEP GUIDE TO INSTALLING A TRELLIS SYSTEM

The trellis system is used to train the vines to grow in a particular direction. Without a trellis, grape vines would simply crawl at ground level, and it would be very difficult to maintain such a vineyard.

1. Planting is usually performed prior to the installation of the trellis system. The trellis system can be installed when the grape vines are two to three feet in length already.

2. Large wooden posts are needed for the trellis system. Post markers are installed in every row and line posts are laid out in the vineyard.

3. To facilitate the installation of the wooden posts, hydraulic augers can be used (the same machines used to install wooden fences). Wooden posts should measure 3.5 inches by 8 feet. The depth of the initial hole should be at least two feet.

4. Since the grape vines have already matured and smaller bamboo stakes have already been used to start training the vines to grow upward, the installation of wooden posts should be done across the rows and in between the vines to avoid any damage to the plants.

5. The areas in between killed rows are generally untilled. In such cases, pilot holes should be created to make the installation of the posts less difficult.

6. You can check the depth of the hole and the length of visible post with a pre-marked measuring stick.

7. After installing the vertical posts across the rows, the H-brace should be prepared next. You still need 3.5 in. x 8 ft. wooden posts. Drill holes into each end of the posts. The depth of each hole should be 2.5 inches. The diameter should be 3/8 of an inch.

8. To make drilling easier, mark the drill bit so you don't exceed the average depth of 2.5 inches. Create the same holes in the vertically-installed wooden poles.

9. Next, place 5-inch brace pins into the vertical poles. Make sure that you insert half of each brace pin. The exposed part of the brace pin will be used to attach the vertical pole to the H-brace.

10. Place the H-brace onto the vertical posts. Drill another 4.5 inches on the outer side of the vertical post and place nine-inch brace pins in the new holes. The remaining exposed part of the pins will be used for the bracing wire later.

11. Run soft bracing wires from one post to another. Splice the bracing wires so that consistent loops are formed for each braced post. Wires should run from the top and bottom of each post (to create a total of two loops).

12. To make the metal loops more secure, use a strong staple gun to secure the wires on the posts.

13. Once the loops are in place, the wires should be twisted tightly around each other to tighten the wire and stabilize the line.

14. After creating a complete anchor system (H-brace + tightened soft bracing wires), it's time to install a high tensile wire on top of the anchor system. Crimping sleeves are needed to lock the high tensile wires into place (here, we are referring to the starting posts and end posts for each row).

15. A single high-tensile wire should be installed in every row. Secure the high-tensile wire with staples. To ensure the durability of the installation, use two staples each time you have to place a top wire on a post.

16. In order to sustain the position of the high-tensile wires, strainers should be placed in between each anchor system.

17. Use a gauge to measure the average tension of the top wire on each row.

18. Tie strings to connect the top wire to the bamboo support on the ground. This will help train the vines to grow upward, toward the secure top wire.

CHECKLIST FOR THE ANNUAL CARE OF GRAPE VINEYEARDS

Follow this checklist to ensure maximum growth and productivity in your vineyard.

March – Initial Pruning

The following are needed for the summer care of a grape vineyard:

1. Repair of the trellis system (includes, but is not limited to, installation of new posts, installing new tensile wires, removal of worn-out bracing wire, etc.).

2. Cordon wires or top wires should be tightened during this time of the year. Use a gauge to check if the tension of each cordon wire is at least 250 pounds. The high-tensile wires can be tightened up to 300 pounds.

3. Some wooden posts may have been infested by crown gall. In such cases, remove the damaged wooden posts or mark the damaged ones for removal after the ocular inspection.

4. Prune the grape vines only if necessary. The viability of the grape buds should be ascertained prior to any pruning activity to ensure maximum harvest later on.

5. Every two years, soil analysis should also be carried out. Soil analysis allows the vineyard owner to discover whether or not the soil's mineral content has already been depleted.

6. The following lines concerns particular pruning practices that should be used during this time of the year depending on the number of dead primary grape buds.

Percentage of Primary Bud Mortality:

0% - 20%. The current pruning technique is working well and should not be adjusted or changed.

20% - 80% mortality. Retain a larger number of buds to compensate for the large mortality of early buds.

More than 80% mortality. Actively growing nodes should be retained. Nodes should be pruned away only if the growth will be pushing against the adjacent grape vine.

April – Installing Vine Protection

1. During this time of the year, weed pests will begin to invade vineyards. Pre-emergent herbicides can be used to protect your growing grape vines.

The timing has to be right in order for the pre-emergent herbicides to work. If you apply the herbicide to early in the year, there is a big chance that the enzyme responsible for its action will be absorbed too deeply into the soil, which reduces the herbicide's effectiveness.

2. Some pruning can be done during April as well. If any pruning is necessary, do it in late April, as this will reduce bud breakage.

3. To protect the vineyard from unnecessary injuries from fungi infections, dormant fungicides should also be applied during this month.

Take stock of the growth of the vines and the spacing of the rows to make sure that the vines are still getting plenty of air circulation and adequate sunlight.

4. Many vineyards install 'deer fences'. These metal fences keep out people and large animals. Electrifying these fences is also a common practice to keep the vineyard safe from foraging animals and human intruders.

5. After pruning the vines, the debris or waste produced by the activity should be gathered and removed from the vineyard.

Don't let the pruning debris stay in the vineyard - keep the rows as clean as possible.

6. If any vines have died, re-plant vines.

7. Inspect the growing vines and check for bug infestations. The two most common pests of the grape vine are the flea beetle and the climbing cutworm.

May – Pest & Fertilizer Management

1. May is the time when additional nitrogen should be added to the soil. Soil sampling can be done so you can see the nitrogen levels in your vineyard.

2. General disease control should also be performed during this time of the year. Watch out for the following:

- Phomopsis (a fungal disease)
- Powdery mildew (a fungal disease)
- Black rot (may be caused by bacteria or fungi)
- Downy mildew (caused by parasitic microbes)

Ocular inspections to detect such problems in your vineyard should be carried out two to three times a year.

3. Don't forget pest management during May. The most common pests in the grape vineyard are:

- Cane borers
- Phylloxera
- Cane gallmaker
- Cane girdler

The following are essential facts about these four common grape vineyard pests:

Cane borer

- Attack the leaves of grape vines.
- The cane borer has a metallic appearance, which makes it easier to spot.
- An adult borer can reach up to 3 inches in length.
- The young of the cane borer are leg-less larvae with flat heads.
- Borers tend to lay eggs before winter. The larvae hatch within the vines and stay there until spring. When spring comes,

the larvae grow significantly in size and molt two times.

- Damage from a cane borer can easily be identified by looking for characteristic borer marks on twigs and vines.

Phylloxera

- Unlike the cane borer, the phylloxera attacks the grape vine root system.

If no proper pest management is performed on a plant that is under attack from a horde of phylloxera bugs, the grape vine can die within a few months.

- In terms of size, the cane borer is a giant compared to the louse-like phylloxera. The phylloxera is almost microscopic in size.

- This species is known to attack the root systems of European grape cultivars and not American grape cultivars. If a European stock has been attacked, it is possible to graft native American stock to avoid similar problems in the future.

- This pest is most dominant in California vineyards, as well as grape vineyards in South America.

The presence of this pest in New Zealand and other countries may be due to accidental transfers (which can occur when grape stocks are imported from other countries and planted on native soil).

Cane gallmaker

- This pest can be found in the eastern region and midwestern region of the United States.

In some areas, the cane gallmaker is considered a major pest and this insect can cause significant problems in grape vineyards if not detected early.

Cane gallmakers reproduce only once every year. As the vineyard owner, it is your task to find these pests before they even reproduce.

- Adults gallmakers measure only 3 millimeters in length. These insects are weevils and have the characteristic short snout of other weevils.

- Like the cane borer, the cane gallmaker lays its eggs just before the winter months and waits in the vine for spring to arrive. Then it begins to molt during early spring.

- The cane gallmaker usually starts laying eggs when individual shoots of grape vines measure at least 25-centimeters in length. They can also lay eggs in vines that are 50-centimeters in length already.

- The female gallmaker will most likely avoid vine nodes that are likely to produce active grape bud clusters.

- During midsummer, a fully grown adult gallmaker will emerge from damaged shoots and will begin feeding on the rest of the vine. Adult gallmakers will continue to emerge from their secret lairs in the vine until September of the same year.

- To spot this pest, look for any swelling in the shoots and round exit holes that newly-emerged adult gallmakers may have created.

Cane girdler

- The cane girdler is a significant pest in grape vineyard because it attacks young shoots instead of mature vines. If left unchecked, a large horde or cane girdlers can drastically reduce the overall grape production of an affected grape vineyard.

- Initially, the cane girdler fed only on the Virginia grape cultivar. In more recent times however, this species has adapted well to the presence of other grape cultivars in US vineyards and has learned how to feed on the young shoots of other grape cultivars.

- Adult girdlers usually attack grape vines when the shoots are thirty to fifty centimeters long. This species accomplishes over-wintering by migrating to the organic trash that can be found in every vineyard (fallen leaves, dead twigs, etc.).

- When adult cane girdler attacks young shoots, shoots tend to bend, and in time, fall to the ground. It is possible to identify the presence of this pest by looking at roughly 'pruned' twigs and shoots.

4. Persistent weed pests must also be taken care of in the month of May. Common systemic herbicides designed for weed pests can be used.

Ocular inspection of the vineyard should be done from row

to row to make sure that no row remains unchecked. It is recommended that an integrated inspection for disease, insect pests, and weed pests be carried out.

5. Water sprouts should be removed from the main vines. Otherwise, additional vines can grow right in front of a mature grape vine. You can keep these water sprouts if the current vine is already damaged or you are expecting some winter damage.

Otherwise, remove the water sprouts. The presence of water sprouts simply means that the plant is extremely healthy and active. If you let the water sprout grow, it will develop into a grape vine that is exactly like the one you have already planted.

6. Another important task during May is shoot thinning or suckering. Start by removing base shoots that are generally undesirable or unnecessary.

Next, remove shoots that are not growing any active fruit clusters. Finally, shoots with fruit clusters should only be removed if there is evidence of disease or pests.

Thinning shoots has several benefits, including:

- The periderm of the new shoots are hardier and more resistant to injury.

- Newly grown buds will mostly likely continue sprouting actual grapes.

- Shoot thinning also reduces the risk of developing serious problems like widespread Botrytis blight.

- Leaf canopy is also spared from fungal diseases.

- Regular watering spray and herbicide application is also more effective because vines are penetrated more effectively.

- Grape quality is improved, which in turn produces better wine.

- Hand harvesting becomes more efficient and less difficult. Thus, you save time and energy during the yearly harvest.

7. Cluster thinning is also done in this month. Cluster thinning is performed to increase the size of grape clusters, especially if you are growing table grape cultivar.

8. After shoot thinning and cluster thinning, the next task is to position the shoots to maintain a narrow single canopy. This

can be done by increasing the height of the catch-wires in the vineyard. If you are using a fixed system, then 'tucking in' the shoots will do.

June & July - Major Pest Management

1. Pest and disease management should be performed on an ongoing basis. In June, check your plants for botrytis. Botrytis is also known as botrytis blight or gray mold (as opposed to related conditions like black mold).

The most common pathogen that causes gray mold is the fungi species Botrytis cinerea. This problem usually emerges when the weather is rainy and cool - the perfect conditions for gray mold.

You can easily spot this problem by looking at the buds and fruits. The presence of gray or partly brown mold is a sure sign that your vines are afflicted with Botrytis blight. In addition to buds and fruits, Botrytis blight can also affect shoots and leaves of the grape vines.

Regular maintenance is the easiest way to protect your grape vines from massive damage from Botrytis blight. Whenever you are doing a routine ocular inspection of your grape vines, carry a small bag with you.

Inspect vines, shoots, and fruits, and remove dead plant parts and place these in the bag. By removing moldy parts of the plant, you are directly suppressing the damaging potential of the pathogen by weakening its hold on individual vines.

If your vines have already suffered from Botrytis blight in the past, it is highly recommended that you avoid the following:
- Misting the foliage
- Syringing
- Overhead watering systems

It is also recommended that proper spacing of each vine be observed to encourage healthy air circulation. Air circulation can drastically increase the risk for different types of molds, not just gray mold.

If the problem with gray mold becomes uncontrollable, you

may want to invest in a good fungicide.

Take note that not all fungicides can be used on grape vines. Each fungicide is registered as being effective for a particular plant and a particular fungi pathogen. So keep this in mind when you are looking for a good brand of fungicide.

2. During this time of the year, additional pests may be found in grape vineyards, including:

- Grasshoppers
- Sphinx moth
- Leafroller
- Leafhoppers
- Japanese beetle
- Rose chafer
- Eight spotted forester
- Grape berry moth

3. Continue weed management throughout this month.

4. It is during this time of year that you can estimate how much you will be harvesting for this year.

This can be done by multiplying the average number of grape clusters for every vine by the weight of an average cluster of grapes. After producing an estimated yield, you can start calling potential buyers.

5. Perform leaf thinning to increase the amount of sunlight that healthy grape clusters are receiving. The ideal time to perform leaf thinning is when the clusters have fully emerged and the fruits have already set.

6. Since active clusters have already formed, it is possible for your vineyard to attract raccoons and different types of birds.

The installation of bird netting should be performed before veraison or the full ripening of the grapes. The cover crop should be removed (through mowing) before any bird netting is installed in the vineyard.

7. The rate of veraison of grape cultivars differ. If you have grapes that have ripened early in the year, it would be a good idea to contact your buyers so you can do a partial harvest and deliver the newly ripened grapes.

8. Full maturation of the grape cultivar can be ascertained by measuring the sugar level in the grapes (using the Brix scale) and by measuring the acidity of the fruit.

9. Vegetation around the vines should be allowed at this point in time.

August – Harvest Season

1. August is harvest time! It is during this time of the year that you should be regularly monitoring and sampling your grapes. A Brix reading of three (more or less) is a sign that the grapes are ready for harvesting.

Daily grape sampling and Brix measurement is recommended. When early cultivars emerge, don't forget to contact your buyers to let them know. Work closely with all your buyers (old and new) so that you will have every opportunity to sell your harvest.

2. The second most important concern during August is the refrigeration and transport services that will handle the freezing and delivery of your grapes. Make sure that you have these prepared.

You have several options: deliver the grapes fresh or deliver the produce in frozen form, in plastic tubs. Wineries are fine with both types of produce (though some would prefer that you deliver fresh grapes instead of frozen grapes).

3. All containers, large and small, should be sanitized properly during and after the harvest and delivery of the grapes. An unsanitary vineyard can produce a myriad of problems such as prematurely fermenting grapes, etc.

4. During this time, you have two main pests to deal with: the grape berry moth and the Asian lady beetle.

5. If your cultivar seems a bit slow in fully maturing in August, you probably have a late-season grape cultivar. This is completely normal and you should just continue with the regular monitoring of the Brix level of the grapes. Don't forget the target reading: you need at least a 3 on the Brix scale to harvest the grapes.

6. Plant analysis and soil analysis should also be carried out during harvest season. Schedule these samplings early in the year; plant analysis is usually performed some months after the first grape blooms.

September – Post-Harvest Work

1. September is the usual harvest month for late-season grape cultivars. If you planted such grape cultivars in your vineyard, be prepared to extend the Brix sampling another month (or at least until mid-month).

2. As the grapes ripen, the Asian lady beetle will remain a potential threat to an easy and uneventful harvest. Keep an eye out for these bugs.

3. Since this is the last month for harvesting, the bird netting that was installed to protect the ripening grapes from raccoons, birds and other small foraging animals should be removed completely.

4. During the post-harvest phase, many vineyards suffer from a sudden infestation of powdery mildew. This condition can be easily detected because you can see grayish or whitish 'powder' on the leaves of the affected vines.

Outdoor crops (not just grapes) are affected by powdery white mildew and the pathogens that cause this problem usually come full force during the late-harvest period.

If left untreated, powdery white mildew can cause the foliage and stems to wither and fall off. Plant tissue (including shoots, buds and stems) can also disintegrate under the relentless advance of the fungi.

To combat this problem, a fungicide made especially for grapevines afflicted with powdery white mildew should be used. The fungicide must be sprayed on all plants, not just those that are affected or are in close proximity to afflicted vines.

It is recommended that vineyard owners start treatment for powdery white mildew even before the regular harvesting season. Once you see small white patches appearing on the foliage of the grape vines, start applying the appropriate fungicide.

5. Herbicides, on the other hand, should also be used to control the pest weed population that also increases post-harvest.

6. If the soil in the vineyard becomes dry post-harvest, proper irrigation should be given to prevent impenetrable soil caps from forming.

7. Since the usable nitrogen in the soil has already been depleted by the current year's crops, organic fertilizer (manure) should be applied to the soil.

The results of the earlier soil sampling (which can be carried out during August) will help you determine how much manure per acre is needed to replenish the depleted nitrogen in the soil.

October – Planning

1. The vineyard owner's job is not done after the first harvest. There is still plenty to do in the vineyard!

Your first task when the month of October rolls in is to reduce the tension of the top wire of your trellis. Repair of the anchor system, wires, and posts should also be done post-harvest, to prepare for the next planting.

2. If you have installed electrified fencing to ward off larger foraging animals like deer, it is time to power down the fence - the grapes have already been sold and foragers won't be too interested in what remains in your vineyard.

3. The irrigation system (which may have been used to moisten the soil post-harvest) should be drained properly.

4. To improve your vineyard's performance next harvesting season, you have to talk to all your buyers and get their feedback on the quality of the cultivar(s) that you have delivered.

Note all of the feedback, positive or otherwise, and use this information to improve your maintenance plan for the season. After getting customer feedback, you should also look back and find out whether or not you were efficient in planting, maintaining and harvesting the cultivars. Note areas in your performance review that needs improving and remember to implement the changes next season.

5. Since the grapes have already been harvest and delivered, it's time to plan for next season!

GUIDELINES FOR SELECTING GRAPE CULTIVARS

Grape cultivars constitute both the brand and product of every vineyard. Some vineyards are known for producing exquisite grapes for white wines, while others are known for producing great cultivars for red wine production, etc.

The type of cultivar you plant will have a large bearing on the success of your vineyard. Here are some guidelines to ensure success when you are selecting the type(s) of grapes to be planted for the first time.

I. What type of cultivar is in high demand in your area? If you live in a region of the country where the demand for wine grapes is high, you wouldn't want to start producing table grapes.

Vineyards should also respond to what the market needs. This will ensure that the profit generated from your yearly produce will be able to cover operational costs and other expenditures tied to keeping your vineyard.

Once you have identified your particular market, you will also be able to identify what type of product your market needs. This will aid in you in preparing the grapes during harvest. For example, the needs of a winery is different from a manufacturing facility that produces grape jams.

You should work closely with your potential market so you

know exactly what they need from your grapes in terms of:

> Color of the grapes
> Aroma of the grapes
> Sugar content
> Acidity level
> Seedless or non-seedless condition

All of these individual characteristics are dependent on the type of cultivar that you have planted in your vineyard. If you produce something that your market really needs, then you will have a very loyal market during the harvest season.

II. Try to make a long-term plan: what particular grape variety will be in short supply in half a decade or more? You can do some research to answer this question. You also need to find out what other vineyards in your surrounding area are producing right now.

III. Your vineyard itself is a key factor when it comes to determining what type of cultivar would be feasible to plant.

Environmental factors like soil quality, consistent weather conditions, and wind conditions all play a part in your vineyard. Your cultivar should be able to withstand or survive all these environmental factors.

IV. As a vineyard owner, you should also have a clear idea of the vigor or growth potential of a particular cultivar that you wish to plant in your vineyard.

Knowledge of plant vigor will give you an idea as to how you should adjust the row spacing of the individual vines. The architecture of your trellis system should also be designed in accordance with your knowledge of the chosen grape cultivar.

Row spacing is such an important factor in a successful vineyard because, as we have discussed in an earlier section of this book, two things can happen when the row spacing is simply inadequate:

- First, if the grape vines are too close together, the productivity of the vineyard will shoot up for a very brief period but will eventually decline because the vines will not be getting enough air circulation and sunlight.

- Secondly, if the grape vines are too far apart, then the vineyard's general productivity per acre is drastically reduced because you have fewer vines per row.

The general layout of the vineyard should be balanced to create maximum yield, but at the same time, reduce potential problems with row spacing.

V. You also need to do some research regarding the winter temperatures in your area. You need a grape cultivar that will be able to withstand the winter months and will suffer from a minimal amount of winter injury.

VI. If you are planning to plant Vitis vinifera species in your vineyard, note that many known variants of this species are not very adaptive to climate conditions in the Midwest.

In such cases, viticulturists have devised several strategies to prevent the mass die-off of Vitis vinifera grape vines.

For example, mounds of extra soil may be place near the vines to prevent too much heat from escaping during the night time. As for the architecture of the vineyard, the trellis system can also be modified so the vines will grow at a lower height.

Is it practical to go to such efforts to plant grape cultivars that have not adapted to your geographical location? The answer is no, it's not practical at all.

If you wish to plant non-adapted cultivars in your vineyard, note that the operating costs will be somewhat higher because you have to exert extra effort to keep the vines alive.

In such cases, the extra effort should only be given by the viticulturist if there are only a few non-adapted vines to take care of. But it is not recommended that you plant such cultivars throughout your vineyard.

VII. Grape cultivars that are adaptive to regions of the country like the Midwest include:

Catawba - This cultivar is used as a table fruit (rather than a wine grape). Berries from this variant is fairly large but the vines tend to produce smaller fruiting clusters.

This is a late-season cultivar that will produce a satisfactory harvest probably mid-September or late-August.

The Catawba variant is capable of producing a large yield if pruning and maintenance is adequate. Catawba is affected primarily by downy mildew and other fungal diseases.

Concord - This type of grape is usually marketed for fruit juice production and wine production.

A seeded cultivar, it is also prone to developing black rot, which is the reason why an adequate systemic herbicide program is required to preserve the vines throughout the budding and ripening periods.

Delaware - The Delaware cultivar is used primarily to produce what is called 'blush wine'. It produces a fairly large yield if tended properly and can also be marketed to wineries producing sparkling wine.

Niagara - The Niagara cultivar is fairly versatile. It can be used as a table grape but can also be used in the production of juices and wines.

Loose fruiting clusters and fewer berries per cluster characterizes the Niagara cultivar. A seeded variety, it has been said that Niagara grapes produce excellent grape juice (which is the reason why it can be marketed to wineries foremost).

Cayuga White - First used by vineyard owners in the year 1972, the Cayuga White variety produces white grapes fit for wine production.

Because of its high vigor, other vine training methods such as the cordon system can be used. This cultivar is usually used to produce dry wines.

Chardonel - A late-season cultivar, the Chardonel is closely related to the grapes that produce Chardonnay wine.

Though the clusters of this cultivar produces fewer grapes and the vines generally produce a moderate yield, the plant itself is fairly resistant to most fungi problems like black rot.

Marquis - If you've been looking for a high-yield grape cultivar for table use, then the Marquis is a good option. First introduced in the year 1996, this cultivar fares well when trained using the cordon system.

VIII. You must also be aware that cultivars are very different from actual grape species. A single species can have as many as one hundred hybrid cultivars.

GRAPE SPECIES & CULTIVARS

The following list sheds light on the different species of grapes grown throughout the World. It will help you determine which species to select, based on its most important characteristics.

Species of Grapes: *V. vinifera*
Native Regions: This species originated from Asia Minor. It's the vitis sensu lato and currently present on all continents except Antarctica.

Characteristics & Vineyard History: The European grape species is popular with vineyards in the Western United States. However, this species, and all its cultivars, are generally prone to attacks from the phylloxera pest. This is the reason why this species is not very popular in the Northeast. V. vinifera grapes have longer growing seasons than other grape species and require a hotter temperature in order to thrive. It does not produce high yields if the region is generally rainy during the months when the grapes are ripening.

Popular Cultivars: Chadonnay, White riesling, Pinot blanc, Pinot gris, Gewurztraminer, Muscat ottonel, Sauvignon blanc, Comtessa, Morio Muscat, Noblessa, Semillon, Siegerrebe, Cabernet sauvignon, Cabernet franc, Merlot, Limberger, Gamay noir, Trollinger, Rotberger, Petite Verdot.

Species of Grapes: *V. rotundifolia, V. acerifolia, V. angulata, V. cordifolia, V. hyemalis, V. incisa, V. muscadina, V. mustagenesis, V. peltata, V. verrucosa.*

Native Regions: All Southern regions of Delaware and Illinois. Northeast Texas. Success in growing these species have also been noted in Washington and Oregon. California is also a good place to plant these grape species.

Characteristics & Vineyard History: These ten species are highly adapted to very humid areas. While this is an advantage to vineyard owners living in the native regions of these species, all are quite susceptible to winter injury (mainly, frost). The lowest temperature that these species can tolerate is zero degrees Fahrenheit. If the temperature drops to about -10 degrees Fahrenheit, widespread winter injuries will occur throughout the vineyard. All the cultivars of these species fare well in areas where there is well-drained soil and swamps. Though these species can tolerate hot summer months, the vines will not grow well if exposed to semi-arid conditions. Unlike *V. vinifera* and all its cultivars, these species are immune to attacks from phylloxera and even nematode invaders.

Popular Cultivars: Triumph, Black beauty, Taraheel, Black fry, Tara, Bountiful, Sweet Jenny, Chief, Supreme, Cowart, Summit, Darlene, Sterling, Dearing, Scuppernong, Delight, Regale, Dixie, Pineapple, Doreen, Noble, Florida, Nesbitt, Florida Fry, Magnolia, Loomis, Fry, Jumbo, Higgins, Janet, Hunt, Ison.

Species of Grapes: *V. labrusca, V. blandi, V. canina, V. ferrunginga, V. latifolia, V. luteola, V. sylvestris virginiana, V. taurina, V. vin. sylvestris americana, V. vulpina.*

Native Regions: Can be found in northeast regions and east regions of the United States.

Characteristics & Vineyard History: All species and cultivars from this line of grapes are also immune to phylloxera attacks. The *V. labrusca* species has been used for many years to produce hybrid grapes that are resistant to pests.

Popular Cultivars: Alexandar, Himrod, Champion, Reliance, Concord, Niagara, Delaware.

Species of Grapes: *V. aestivalis, V. nortoni, V. lincecumii, V. bicolor.*

Native Regions: These species can be found in numerous ranges, from the northern hemisphere all the way to the continent of Africa.

Characteristics & Vineyard History: It is said that these species are immune to Pierece's disease, a devastating condition caused by bacterial pathogens that are spread mainly by the insect pest *leafhopper*. One of the negative traits of these species is that they generally do not produce hardy root systems..

Popular Cultivars: Norton, Americana.

Species of Grapes: *V. riparia, V. amara, V. callosa, V. colombina, V. concolor, V. cordifolia, V. cordifolia riparia, V. dimidiata, V. illinoensis, V. incisa, V. intermedia, V. missouriensis, V. montana, V. odoratissima, V. palmata, V. popufolia, V. rubra, V. tenuifolia, V. virginiana, V. virgniensis.*

Native Regions: These species and cultivars are widely distributed throughout the states in the US. From Tennessee to Manitoba, to the Rockies, these species are truly adaptive.

Characteristics & Vineyard History: These grape stocks have been know to withstand up to -60 degrees Fahrenheit without suffering serious winter injury. Riparia varieties are ideal for creating hardy hybrids. However, the cultivars tend to bloom early in the year but ripen late in the season..

Popular Cultivars: Riparia Martin, *et. al.* (No English counterparts to the original French names of these grape stocks have been created).

PLANTING THE GRAPES

Before you plant your first grape stocks, your vineyard should have already been prepared beforehand.

Some tasks, such as the installation of the trellis system can be performed after the stock-planting. Other tasks, such as soil sampling, adding manure, and row spacing, should be done beforehand.

Ordering the Grape Stocks

Unlike other crops, grapes require a longer period of time in order to produce viable cuttings or grape stock.

Many popular variants like the Cynthiana have to be ordered 12 to 24 months in advance prior to the date of the actual planting. Keep this in mind when planning out your first planting.

Rooted cuttings are the best option when you are planting grape vines for the first time.

You can experiment with creating hybrids later on, but for the first attempt, cuttings with excellent root systems should be used. Also, the vines from where the grape stock are coming should be at least a year old.

Before doing anything, inspect all the grape stocks that are delivered to your vineyard. The stock itself should be no thinner than 3/8 of an inch; the main stem of the stock should be as thick as a regular pen.

The roots on the other hand, should not be dry, nor should it be overly wet. Root systems that are moist and appear healthy are a good sign that the nursery that you had contacted really knows how to take care of grape stock.

Note that if any problems are detected with the newly delivered stock, you should contact your supplier immediately to ask for replacement stock.

Pruning New Stocks

New grape stocks are usually trimmed by vineyard owners to just one sturdy stem or cane. Each cane should have at least three buds (but no more than four active buds). All existing shoots that may have grown should be clipped off neatly with a sterile nipper.

Now, if the grape stocks arrived at a time that you are unable to immediately transplant them to the ground, you must store the cuttings in a cool, dry location. The roots and canes must be kept moist with moderate misting/watering until the actual planting date.

If you have access to a cold storage facility, you can place your grape cuttings there, too. The temperature should be above the normal freezing point for plants.

If freezing the new stocks is not a viable option, then you can simply create a temporary trench in your vineyard where the stocks can be kept. The trench should be created in an area where there is plenty of natural shade from surrounding vegetation.

The trench must be shallow enough for easier retrieval of all the cuttings. Mark the individual spaces for each of the grape cuttings as each cutting also requires sufficient air circulation in order to survive.

The roots of the plants must be covered in organic mulch to protect from invading insects and to maintain a steady temperature. Organic mulch also provides a continuous source of plant nutrients through decomposition.

To facilitate the temporary planting of the grape cuttings, you will need a regular hydraulic auger. Augers that normally produce holes with a depth range of eight to ten inches are recommended for this task.

It is important to punch neat, loose holes into the ground. Glazed holes should not be used for grape cuttings. If your vineyard generally has a lot of clay content, metal bits welded unto the hydraulic auger can help break down tough soil.

Planting Period

During the actual planting operation, you have the choice of using mechanical planting equipment or manually planting each of the grape stocks.

Due to issues of practicality and labor time, many vineyard owners opt for mechanical planting. However, it has been reported that mechanical planting produces a larger percentage of inaccurate row spacing compared to manual planting with the aid of pre-marked rows.

On the other hand, it has also been said that the accuracy at which plant stocks can be transplanted to pre-marked rows depends on the equipment that was used during the planting as well as land conditions.

During the planting, the roots of the grape cuttings should be kept moist. Do not allow the root systems to dry out completely, as this can adversely affect the survival rate of the young cuttings.

There are two easy methods to keep the root systems of the cuttings moist throughout the planting period:

Submerge the roots in buckets of water. Since the stocks will be planted, the extra water will not harm the plants.

The stocks can be placed on the ground but they have to be protected by a layer of tarp to slow down the evaporation of moisture from the roots.

Preserving the Root System

Regardless of the planting technique that is being utilized in your vineyard, one clear principle should never be neglected: the holes that you are digging (either manually or with the help of a hydraulic auger) should be large enough to easily accommodate the single cane and the entire root system of each of the grape stocks.

By digging holes with an adequate diameter, you are minimizing or completely eliminating the need to perform some premature pruning on the grape stocks. Any more pruning after removing the shoots and excess grape buds can also affect the growth and survival rate of the grape cuttings.

Before inserting the cutting into the hole, you must first manually spread out the roots (do it gently, so as to not break any of the smaller roots), and lower it carefully into the hole. Soil must then be applied around the roots. Water the newly planted stock immediately.

Spring Planting

When is the best time to plant grape cuttings? Based on the experience of many vineyard owners around the country, the best time of the year to plant grapes is during spring, just after the last vestiges of winter frost have finally disappeared.

It is recommended that the irrigation and trellis systems be installed prior to the planting. Nevertheless, many vineyard owners still opt to install the trellis system after planting to create more accurate spacing for the wooden posts.

After planting the grape stock, inspect the soil around the single cane. Is there a visible depression around the plant? If there is, adjust the level of the soil by adding more soil around the stock and lightly patting the added soil to increase its firmness.

This is done to prevent the pooling of excess water, fertilizers, and pesticides around the vines. If such pooling happens and the event goes undetected, vines can suffer from chemical burns from the concentrated chemicals directly touching the plant tissue.

Fall Planting

Can grapes be planted during the fall season? The answer is a mixed yes-no.

Yes, if you have access to cuttings of species that are very hardy during the wintertime and is resistant to winter injury that may stunt grape production during the growth season. No, if you have access only to summer-loving grape cultivars.

Another potential problem with fall planting is the availability of the grape stocks.

Some nurseries may have the species or cultivar that you are looking for, but the nurseries may not be ready to deliver for a few months. It is common knowledge that nurseries generally do not prepare cuttings as the colder months roll in.

It is still possible to get some grape stock of a viable cultivar, but you may have to order it many months in advance, and the nursery of your choice may have to set aside some special cuttings so they can deliver before the planting date.

Here some very important reminders for fall planting:

The grape stocks must be in dormant condition prior to planting. Dormancy can be achieved by placing the grape cuttings in cold storage prior to the actual planting.

To protect the vine from frost, extra mulch (organic or otherwise) must be added to each of the planted stocks.

Grape stocks that are planted during the fall season do not require as much water as stocks that are planted during spring.

The First Two Years

After successfully planting your first grape stocks, your main focus during the first two years of vine growth is protecting your vines from insect pests. Management of fertilizers is also important, as this has a direct bearing on the growth rate of your new plants.

ORGANIC FARMING & DISEASE MANAGEMENT

One of the biggest obstacles to maintaining a healthy vineyard is vine disease, which can be caused either by bacteria (usually spread by invading insects like leaf-hoppers and leaf-rollers) and common fungi.

Different grape species have different levels of resistance against diseases.

European vinifera species – Unfortunately, pure vinifera cultivars are not resistant to pests and diseases present on American soil. This is the reason why the use of pure European grape cultivars may cause many problems during the growth and ripening seasons.

To protect vinifera species from common diseases like black rot, regular and systemic application of fungicides can be explored. However, the increased risk for developing many diseases and attracting many pests can also raise the operation costs of you vineyard.

American species (V. labrusca, etc.) - Are native American grape cultivars resistant to pests and diseases? Not really - the resistance level of each cultivar varies. Some cultivars are resistant to black rot and other types of mold, but may be susceptible to insect attacks.

In terms of solid resistance to grape diseases caused by fungi or bacteria, two cultivars stand out: the Norton cultivar and the

Edelweiss cultivar. Grape-bunch problems (also caused by molds) is dealt with easily by the V. rotundifolia species.

Now, one of the main issues that organic grape growers have to contend with is disease management.

While many organic growers prefer using natural methods for controlling diseases and pests (like growing healthy populations of beneficial insects in the vineyard), a large percentage of these growers still make use of fungicides and herbicides with active ingredients like sulfur.

While it is true that these agents are considered "organic" because the base material has been acquired through mining, it still remains that the accumulation of sulfur, for instance, can cause plant tissue damage in the long term.

Plant tissue damage isn't the only problem in this respect, because excess sulfur in the soil can also decimate beneficial insects that are naturally controlling the population of weevils and borers in the vineyard.

The solution? If you wish to use organic methods in growing and maintaining grapes, you must select a grape cultivar that has a high resistance to sulfur. Because sooner or later, the plants will require regular applications of mineral-based fungicide and that will most likely cause damage to the plants later on.

Another option is using fungicides that have been created with copper sulfate and lime. This alternative fungicide, also called the Bourdeaux mix, can still cause damage at very high temperatures; it is merely an alternative that aims to reduce the potential risk for plant damage.

SUMMING UP

Find the Best Land to Establish Your Vineyard
The best asset of any grape vineyard is the land itself. The type of soil, mineral content, and the environmental conditions that are present in the area all play a part in maintaining a healthy and productive vineyard.

This is the reason why you should be very careful when picking out the land that you will later transform to a full-sized vineyard.

Different grape cultivars require different types of soil, but generally, moist, loose soil with lots of loam and organic matter is a good choice for grapes. Soil that is dense with clay may not be the best option for any grape cultivar because the excess clay may cause problems with the root system of the vine.

When picking out a likely site for your new grape vineyard, first inquire about the soil's drainage. If the soil does not drain well, then the site is *not* fit for growing grapes. After discovering the soil's drainage, next inquire about equally important environment conditions like the average wind speed and the weather.

Many cultivars thrive in hot and humid locations - not semi-arid land. Unless you want to plant a cultivar that is known to have a high tolerance of semi-arid conditions, *do not* make use of land that is semi-arid.

Wind speed is also important because it will help you determine what design would be best for your vineyard. Winter temperatures are important too; often grape cultivars are unable to tolerate temperatures below -10 degrees Fahrenheit, though some cultivars are extremely hardy against frost (surviving up to -60 degrees Fahrenheit).

Primary Soil Sampling Is a Must

Site selection is such an important step in the establishment of your first vineyard. In fact, it is highly recommended that you perform a *soil sampling* before transforming any property into a vineyard.

Are grapes very fickle about the type of soil they are planted in? Not really - but remember, your main goal as an aspiring grape grower is to produce a maximum yield on your first harvest. If the soil is not ideal, or not even close to ideal, there is a big chance that your grape vines will suffer from lack of nutrients, poor anchorage, inadequate soil drainage, etc.

A little more about soil drainage: in order to maintain a very productive vineyard, the *internal* soil drainage and *surface* soil drainage should be efficient. The looseness of the soil is also an important factor in proper vine growth. Drainage and soil density both play roles in nurturing a well-formed root system.

The root system of grape vines require thirty to forty inches of loose, nutrient-rich soil before the denser layers of the soil are reached. Any less might stunt the growth of a wide root system, which is essential for proper growth. If you can find a site that is both sandy and rich in organic matter (loamy soil), you're on your way!

Once you get the results of the soil sampling, you can compare the results to our own list of the ideal properties of vineyard soil:

Soil pH level - 5.5 to 6.8
Organic matter content - 3%
Phosphorous level - 50 pounds/acre
Potassium level - up to 300 pounds/acre

Magnesium content - up to 250 pounds/acre
Zinc content - up to 10 pounds/acre
Boron content - 2 pounds/acre

Organic Fertilizers Are Essential To Grape Growth

Organic techniques in growing grape cultivars have steadily risen in popularity these past few years. The use of organic fertilizers or animal manure is recommended during establishment, the growth season, and the post-harvest.

Manure is a natural source of usable nitrogen, which makes it an ideal organic fertilizer. The type of manure you end up needing will depend on the amount of nitrogen, phosphorous, and potassium your vineyard soil needs.

The following is a summary of the nutrient and moisture content of the most common manures:

Dairy cattle manure, swine manure, and beef cattle manure have the highest amount of moisture at 80%.

Broiler litter manure, broiler layer manure, and broiler pullet manure have the highest amounts of potassium, nitrogen and phosphorous.

If your soil need lots of potassium, you may want to use another type of organic fertilizer - cut tobacco stalks. Cut tobacco stalks have 70 pounds of potassium per ton but have the least amount of moisture at 20%.

Note that additional nutrients that are added to the soil during the establishment period will be depleted as the grape vines mature and grow fruiting clusters. This is the reason why application of manure is performed during ripening and after the first harvest season. This is done to prepare for the next planting season.

Temporary & Permanent Cover Crops

Establishment is the stage in vineyard design and preparation where the layout of the entire vineyard and the *soil* is prepared for the actual planting of the grape stock.

Cover crops are needed to keep the loose soil of the vineyard from eroding significantly. The entire vineyard should have loose soil, but the soil surrounding the rows of grapes should be resistant to erosion.

In addition to preventing too much soil erosion from taking place, cover crops are also planted in grape vineyards to ensure that *weed pests* are controlled. Otherwise, weed pests would simply *thrive* in the soil surrounding the grape vines. Before a permanent cover crop can be planted, a temporary cover crop should be installed first.

First, measure the pH level or acidity of the soil and add ground limestone to adjust the pH level to the desired range (vineyard soil can be alkaline or acidic, depending on the region of the country and the surrounding waterways and other natural formations).

Next, add some nutrients to the soil. The amount of manure or fertilizers you will add to the soil is dependent on the results of the soil sampling (which is done before establishment).

Finally, drop-seed plants like Sudan grass so you will have a temporary cover crop. The planting of temporary cover crop can be done during the summer months. When it is time to grow the permanent cover crop, you will need to mow the Sudan grass and plant perennial rye or similar plants.

Don't Forget Row Positioning

Vineyard design is part art and part science.

While some aesthetic considerations can be given during the overall layout of the vineyard, measurement of the rows and the *positioning* of the rows are also of utmost importance. Several environment factors should be taken into consideration when figuring out the positioning or the direction of the rows:

1. The amount of natural sunlight that the area regularly receives on a daily basis.
2. The steepness of the land (slope).
3. The average wind speeds in the area.

Proper row positioning will ensure that your grape vines will not be troubled by insufficient sunlight, poor air circulation and damage from strong winds. Rows should be placed parallel (not against) the general wind direction.

Now, if you are having problems with the natural shade from surrounding vegetation in your area, planting rows should be positioned to run from the north to the south.

The individual spacing of the grape vines should be close together to increase the surface area that can absorb the available sunlight. If proper row positioning and spacing is not accomplished, fungal diseases and stunted growth can result.

Which Vineyard Layout Is The Best?

After deciding on the *row positioning* and measuring your rows for the best *row spacing*, it is now time to map out the entirety of the vineyard layout.

And at this point in time, you have to choose between two specific orientations - the square layout and rectangular layout. For beginning vineyard keepers, the rectangular layout is a good choice for two reasons:

First, the rectangular layout offers a higher potential yield per acre than the square layout. Rows of actively budding grape vines will be longer, and you're getting more grape clusters per row than in a square layout.

Second, the rectangular layout allows the vineyard owner to inspect and maintain his new vineyard with ease. Farming equipment and vehicles can traverse the new vineyard with little difficulty and fewer turns, too. A vineyard that does not necessitate too many turns is considered an efficient, manageable vineyard.

While a rectangular layout will most certainly help your vineyard increase its yield during harvesting season, note that the *soil* must be able to handle the extra load. Rectangular vineyards have longer rows; some rows can reach up to 700 feet in length.

Heavy soils are capable of handling this type of load (plus a well-supported trellis system). Rows that are longer than 700 feet will fare better with sprinkler irrigation systems (rather than a more traditional drip irrigation system).

Roll Up Your Sleeves For Vine Pruning Work in March

March is the official start of your duties as a vineyard owner. Maintenance work, pest management and more. Here is a breakdown of the things that you have to take care of in March:

1. If you have installed the trellis system during the establishment period, it is time to look over at the wooden posts and high tensile wires to see if these are still fit to train and support growing vines.

Using a commercial wire tension gauge should be able to help you determine the tension of the wires. The optimum tension of the top wires is 250 pounds. Try to adjust the wires to come close to this ideal number (you can even go up as far as 300 pounds if you used a quality tensile wire).

After re-adjusting the tension of the high tensile wires, inspect the wooden posts (if you used wooden posts) to see which ones need to be replaced. Soft bracing wires that have been looped across the wooden bracing should also be inspected and replaced, if needed.

2. If you have already planted your grape cuttings last year, your vines should have reached a good size by March of the next year. Should you perform pruning?

Yes, but only if you really need to do it. If there is zero to twenty percent bud mortality on the vines, you don't have to change anything with your pruning. If there is twenty to eighty percent mortality, then fewer buds should be cut off to maintain a constant yield per acre. If more than eighty percent of the buds are lost, prune only if the vine is coming close to pushing against the next plant.

3. Soil sampling should be carried out to monitor the mineral levels in the soil.

Meet the Four Pests of the Grape Vineyard

Believe it or not, grape species have their own pests to contend with, especially during the growth and ripening seasons. It is essential that you are acquainted with the most lethal and most common of these pests, so that you will know when your vineyard is under attack. The three most common pests of grapes are:

Cane borers

Phylloxera

Cane gallmaker

The ***cane borer*** is known for causing significant damage to the stems and leaves of the grape vine. This pest sports a flat, metallic appearance, which should make detecting much easier. Evidence of its activity can also be seen on the vines. U sually there are two holes adjacent to each other on the surface plant tissue. These holes are entrance and exit holes.

The ***phylloxera*** pest focuses on decimating the all-important root system of the grape vine. Once a horde of phylloxera has taken hold of a certain part of a vineyard, vine mortality is high if no intervention is performed. Detection is much harder with ocular inspections because phylloxera bugs are nearly microscopic. This pest is well-known in grape vineyards in the California region.

The ***cane gallmaker*** is a pest in the U.S., particularly in the Midwestern region. Once adult cane gallmakers have reached your vineyard, it is possible that a whole generation of new gallmakers will be hatched after winter. Gallmakers are only 3 mm. in size, which makes them hard to spot. Try to spot these pests during mid-summer when adult gallmakers are most active.

The Benefits of Thinning Shoots

Grape vineyards won't be as productive and healthy if pruning and *thinning* operations are not carried out on a regular basis. Suckering or thinning of the vine's shoots creates many advantages, including:

1. The outer layer of the plant tissue will become hardier and more resistant to common diseases and pests.

2. A large percentage of the remaining buds on the 'counted' shoots will sprout actual fruiting clusters, as opposed to just

dropping off or drying up during the growth season.

3. Shoot thinning also increases a grape species' resistance to fungal diseases, such as black rot or powdery mildew.

4. When shoot thinning is adequate, the efficiency of the irrigation system is increased. If you are spraying fungicides and herbicides, you would also be able to cover more surface area per acre.

5. Since grape vines have fewer shoots to support, the grape clusters would produce bigger berries and these clusters would be less prone to grape cluster diseases.

6. Fewer shoots also means harvesting would be much easier, because visibility and manageability of the vines is improved.

In addition to shoot thinning, *cluster thinning* should also be carried out. This is done to increase the average cluster size for every vine. The size of a grape cluster is important when you are producing table grapes for the local market.

The Secret to Selecting a Winning Cultivar

In addition to having a good vineyard layout and an excellent disease management plan, it is also *essential* that you pick out a winning cultivar to plant in your vineyard.

Not every grape cultivar is suitable for every state and region in the United States and not every cultivar can be marketed to every town.

So here are some tips to get you started on your search for that one grape cultivar that will make your vineyard a complete success:

1. The first step is to find out what your local market actually needs. There are many market niches that you can explore. Vineyards can supply grapes to juice manufacturers, large grocery chains, wineries, etc. You can offer your market frozen grapes, fresh grapes, grape concentrate, and grape juice. You can offer exquisite red wine grapes that will be used to manufacture excellent wine. If your grape cultivar has large clusters, you can offer fine table grapes, too.

2. After establishing the market demand *now*, try to think of the demand for the long term. What cultivars are in short

supply in your area? You can respond to your market this way as well.

3. And finally, try combining your market data with the results of your annual soil sampling and ask yourself this important question: what marketable grape cultivar will fare well in my vineyard?

APPENDIX 1

Grape Growing Information

Although there are many other uses for these delectable fruits, grapes are the basis for most of the world's wine. About seventy-one percent of grapes from around the world are used for wine making, twenty-seven percent are used as fresh fruit, and the remaining two percent of the grapes are used in the form of dry fruit.

There are other types of fruits that are used to create wines, but it is the grape that may just be the perfect fruit for wine making. Grapes contain the right properties to produce wine. Such characteristics of grapes include naturally-high amounts of fermentable sugar, strong flavors, and color in the skins. Grape species have also been refined to deliver the utmost in aroma and flavor. Typically, grape juices are prepared from *Vitis labrusca* grapes, which are a grape species that is native to the Americas, because these grapes have loose skin that can be easily peeled off. *Vitis vinifera* grapes, which is a species of grape that is native to Europe and East and Central Asia, but has been planted all over the world, have a tight skin and can also be used for the production of wine. Grapes are also highly nutritional. They are a rich source of carbohydrates, protein, healthy fats, and they are cholesterol-free.

Although smaller then the productive vineyards all over the

world, many people have succeeded in growing their own grapes at home and even in producing their own wine. Although the time it takes to tend to a small flourishing vineyard is great, the techniques to grow healthy grapevines is minimal. Home grape growers start their vineyards by finding a spot in their yard that possesses optimal conditions in which to successfully grow grapes. First, the area must have good exposure to sunlight and good drainage. After a good rainfall, examine the area you wish to grow your grapes for standing water. Standing water is a good indication that the area does not have sufficient drainage. Planting your vineyard on a slope will also provide the drainage needed to sustain grapevines. A slope can also reduce the grapevine's exposure to heat or cold depending on its orientation. For example, in the cooler regions of the Northern Hemisphere, grapevines benefit from being planted on south facing slopes which offers exposure to a fair amount of heat and sunlight. Tending a vineyard will require daily care. Plant your vineyard where it can be easily accessed during the growing season for pruning, weeding and pest control. You should also make sure that tools and water are easily accessible as well.

Once you have the perfect location for your vineyard, you will need to prepare the soil and construct the trellis. Grapevines are a large plant that and are unable to sustain the weight of the grape clusters it produces. In the wild, grapevines can be found growing on structures like poles and fences. Grapes are perennial plants and therefore it will be about three years before you are able to harvest your first crop. Therefore it is very important to have a sturdy trellis that will last.

Once you are able to harvest your crop, you will be able to make your own wine. The amazing thing about grapes is that the soil and the area in which the grapes are grown will have a significant impact on the taste of the wine thereby making your wine truly unique.

APPENDIX 2

Growing Grapes at Home

Growing grapes at home is not that much different from how they are grown in a large vineyard. The only real difference is space. There are several facets to growing healthy grapevines that need to be considered by both large vineyards and the home grower. The most important aspect of all these is tending to the vines. This will entail soil preparation, water, sunlight, pruning, and pest control. For many home grape growers, it is the pruning and the pest control that can be the most tedious.

Put simply, pruning is cutting away plant growth to encourage more growth. How the grapevine is pruned depends a lot upon the type of grapes that are being grown. Since hybrid grape varieties were developed to be hardier during the winter and more resistant to diseases, they tend to produce less foliage then the traditional types of grapevines. Grapevines need to be pruned to remove the previous years fruiting canes or spurs. Grapes are only produced on shoots growing from one-year-old canes. Therefore, healthy new canes must be produced by the vine every year. If too much of the vine is pruned back, more shoots will grow on the vine, which in turn, produces more crop and foliage. But this is actually a disadvantage since increased foliage on a vine results in a shady canopy, and this provides a bad environment for the fruit to ripen. The home grape grower has to be careful when pruning to avoid any unnecessary injury to the plant. When removing year-old shoots, a hand pruner can be used effectively. Larger wood on the vine should be cut with either a lopper or a handsaw.

The home grape grower spends a lot of their time dealing with pests like insects, birds and even deer. There are a large number of insects, like grape berry moths, grape leafhoppers, Japanese beetles, and rose chafers that would love to dine on a delicious grapevine. Insecticides can be used to control insect infestation but typically, grapevines can withstand a small amount of insect damage. It is only necessary to control insects when a large portion of the leaf area or the fruit itself is threatened.

Birds, on the other hand, can be much more destructive. A flock of birds can devastate a crop of grapes but, on the bright side, a large flock of birds is easier to scare away than individual birds. Home grape growers can control birds by installing a physical barrier, like a net, over all of the vines. But it has to be taken down before the winter or ice could form on it and damage the vines. Home grape growers can also use visual repellents such as aluminum pie plates, artificial hawks, owls, or snakes. Odor repellents are something that are very effective when it comes to controlling deer. In early spring when shoots are just emerging from the vine and food sources are scarce, home grown vineyards are extremely tempting for the deer. Home grape growers can also use the scent of a human, dog hair, or soap to scare off unwanted birds. Additionally, the scent of coyotes can also be used since coyotes are natural predators to deer.

APPENDIX 3

How to Grow Grape Vines in the Right Soil

Growing vines in the right soil is the most pivotal feature of grape growing. The type of soil, its mineral, content and the environmental conditions all play an extremely important role in the health and productivity of the grape vine. Before you plant your grape vines you should have your soil analyzed. Adding nutrients to soil that is lacking is easy, but removing unwanted excess nutrients is nearly impossible. Grape vines are fairly adaptable and don't need much to feed on, meaning they do well in rich, highly organic soils. A positive aspect of growing grapes vines that do not require excessive amounts of nutrients is that a lack of nutrients within the soil will help prevent excessive weed growth. But if your soil test is showing too much nutrient deficiency, you should look to a professional for advice on how to establish good soil for your grape vines. If the wrong adjustments are made to the soil, it could have significant impact on your vines, resulting in excessive unwanted vine and leaf growth in some regions. Something that should also be measured is the soil's pH level. The soil can be alkaline or acidic depending on the region of the country you are growing your grape vines in and the surrounding waterways and other natural formations. A pH that is between 6.0 and 6.5

is perfect for grape vine nutrient intake. You may need to incorporate lime if your soil is acidic meaning that the pH is lower then 6.0. If your soil is basic, or higher then 7.0, you may need to find rootstock that has been adapted to limestone soil conditions.

It may be necessary to add fertilizer to the soil during the time in which the grapes are ripening and after the first harvest season. The nutrients within the soil will be depleted as the grape vine matures and produces fruit. The use of organic fertilizer like manure has risen among grape growers for many different reasons. One reason is that manure is a natural source of usable nitrogen. The type of manure you need depends upon the amount of nitrogen, phosphorous and potassium your vineyard soil requires.

The nutrients within the soil are not the only requirements needed for growing a healthy grape vine. The soil must also supply good anchorage for the vine and provide proper drainage. Grape vines that are grown in soil that has too many nutrients and water go "vegetative". This means that the grape vines will return to leaf growth and will stop producing fruit. Grape vines do not like to sit in puddles and will not grow well in really wet areas. The most established vine yards are well known for excellent drainage. A need for good drainage is one of the many reasons why many vineyards are planted on hillsides. Not only do steep hillsides aid in the drainage of the crop, they also are typically low in nutrient or organic matter due to years of erosion. In addition to a trellis, the grape vine's root system requires ample anchorage from the soil as well in order to support this large plant. They require about thirty to forty inches of loose soil in order to establish a wide root system.

APPENDIX 4

How to Plant and Grow a Successful Grape Vine

Doesn't the thought of relaxing with a bottle of great tasting wine sound luxurious? The thought of sipping on wine that you made *yourself* sounds even better. Planting and growing a successful grape vine is not as complicated as it might seem, and it is the first step in making this dream a reality.

It is up to you to decide how large you want your vineyard to be. If you are just getting started it is a good idea to plant only a few vines. And by a "few", I mean ten. It takes about ten vines to make homemade wine since most homemade wines are made in five- gallon batches. You can obtain year old bare-rooted dormant grape vines from a nursery to start off with. Typically, these vines have been grown by the nursery in their fields. The vines are usually sold in early spring which is a good climate for grape vine planting. The early spring rains will benefit your grape vines and give them a chance to settle in before the growing season begins. But until your vines are ready to be planted, keep the vines moist by spraying them with water.

Planting your vines is quite easy and straightforward. You will need to dig a hole large enough to contain the root system. The buds on the vine should not be covered with soil. Gently hold your vine in the hole while you tap the soil down lightly.

This allows any remaining air pockets to be removed from the soil. If you leave a slight depression around the base of the vine, it makes it easier to water them. After the vine is well planted in the soil, you do not need to water the dormant vines if the soil is damp.

After your vines begin to show signs of life you will need to make sure that your soil remains moist. Sometimes if you get a few good soaking showers, you may not have to water your vines. But if the rainfall in your area is weak, you will need to add water to your vines. Sandy soils need to be watered more often. Clay-based soils need to be watered less often since clay absorbs and retains water longer. With any kind of soil, proper soil drainage is required. With the proper drainage, you do not need to worry about too much rain soaking your vines.

Another aspect of growing a successful grape vine is ensuring that your vines get the right amount of sunlight and air flow. You should not plant your grape vines near trees or structures that can block sunlight and prevent air circulation. In order for plants to undergo photosynthesis, they need sunlight. Photosynthesis is the process that converts carbon dioxide into sugar. It is the sugar within the grapes that becomes alcohol after fermentation. As a result of poor air circulation and too little sunshine, grapes can suffer from fungus disease problems.

Growing a successful grape vine can be a reality for you. Be prepared to give your vineyard year-round attention. It can take up to three years for a grape vine to produce a crop of grapes but, when you have put the time and effort into your vines, the rewards from your first group of grapes will be that much sweeter.

APPENDIX 5

How to Tend to a Grape Vine Growing on a Trellis

Grape vines will naturally grow on a variety of structures like fences, trees or walls. Therefore it is important to establish a well-constructed structure that your grape vines can use as an anchor. A trellis system is important because grape vines cannot support the weight of a full harvest by themselves.

There are many different ways to build a trellis. Some trellises are built for functionality while others are meant to add to the landscape of the home. They can be simple or complex, and you can build it yourself or contract the job out to professionals. It all depends on the taste of the grape grower. A trellis can come in an array of different shapes and sizes in order to suit the needs of the grape grower. They can be made out of a variety of different materials such as iron, pre-treated wood, stainless steel, PVC pipe, or aluminum. The height of the trellis depends on the area where the grapes are growing. Shorter trellises are used in colder climates, since a trellis that is shorter has a better chance of withstanding winter weather. It also makes it easier for the grape grower to prepare the grape vine for winter. Taller trellises can be used in warmer climates. Shorter trellises use posts that are about three feet high while larger trellises require a post that is about eight feet high. While every trellis system is different, there is one thing that they all have in common - they must be sturdy and well made. Since a grape vine usually takes a few years to produce any grapes, the trellis system is going to be in place for a while.

The trellis system should be placed in the yard so that the grape vines will be exposed to a good amount of sunlight and good air movement. Natural sunlight and good air movement are huge factors in ripening the grapes and controlling grape diseases. After you have found the best location for your trellis, you should cement the posts that will support the trellis into the ground. Some grape growers secure their trellis posts by using catch wires anchored to the ground or by placing another much shorter post set in the ground next to the main post. The posts should be set into the ground about eight feet apart. Two rows of galvanized steel wire should be run between the posts. The first wire row runs along the bottom of the posts about three inches from the ground. The second wire needs to run along the top of the posts. A staple gun can be used to staple the wires in place.

As soon as your grape vines starts growing, you will want to start training them to grow on the trellis. This can take years. The main shoot that is growing should be tied vertically to the trellis. You can use string to do this. String will not damage the shoot like wire could. Grape vines grow very slowly, and after the next dormant period, two shoots from either side of the main shoot should be tied horizontally to the trellis. These shoots will serve as the base for the fruit.

APPENDIX 6

The Best Grapes for Growing a Successful Vineyard

Under the California sunlight is not the only place where you can grow a successful vineyard. Nowadays, you can grow grapevines just about anywhere. Since grapevines are naturally adaptable, even areas with extreme climates are now considered suitable for grape growing. Beginners should start off with a grape variety that does particularly well in their particular area or growing zone.

When deciding on a grape variety, remember that your location will have everything to do with your grape growing experience. Did you know that a grape variety that is grown in California will taste much different than that same variety grown in France? That is because soil and weather conditions contribute to the wines specific personalities. You can find out which varieties of grapes grow well in your area by talking to local vintners.

There are over five thousand different types of grape varieties including hybrids. Grape growers who live in areas where the growing season is shorter are limited to the hybrid grape varieties. Grapevines have been bred to last through cooler climates and to be more resistant to disease. But, it is the climate condition in your area that will mostly determine the varieties of grapes that you can grow successfully. Although grape hybrids can grow in cooler conditions, not every grape variety flourishes in every region of the world. You will still need to know the length of your growing season to determine what variety of grape will work best for you. The growing season is the average number of frost-free days. Some of the different grape varieties require longer growing seasons to fully ripen.

Wine grapes are all the same species known as *vitis vinifera*. However, within this species, there are hundreds of cultivars that vary in their characteristics. *Vitis vinifera* grapes are used for the production of wine because they have a tight skin perfect for making wine. It is the species that yields over ninety-nine percent of the world's wines. There are also red grapes and white grapes. Both types can be used to make wine. Some red grape varieties include Merlot, Cabernet Sauvignon, and Syrah. Some of the white grape varieties include Chardonnay, Riesling, Sylvaner and Chenin Blanc. *Vitis vinifera* grapes come from the Mediterranean region, southwestern Asia, Spain, and central Europe. American grapes originated from the *Vitis labrusca*, and are found in Canada and the eastern United States. Wine grapes are smaller in comparison to other types of grapes and usually seeded. They have thick skins, which is what is why they are so desirable since much of the aroma in wine comes from the skin. The grape species that are used for wine also tend to be very sweet. When these grapes are harvested, their juice is about twenty-four percent sugar by weight.

And while seventy-one percent of the world's grapes are used for making wine, there are many other reasons to grow grapes. Grapes are also used for eating and as a dry fruit. They can be made into jelly, vinegar, candy, grape seed extract, seed oil, and jam.

ABOUT THE AUTHOR

Dr. Andrea Scarsi was born in the mainland of Venice, Italy, in 1955. At fifteen he begins practicing yoga, spiritualism and telepathy; at eighteen, after a motorbike accident, he begins contacting and visiting other dimensions.

At twenty-four, on his first trip to India, he consciously enters the world of meditation guided by his Spiritual Master Osho, receiving the title and name of Swami Prem Sandesh, and a forty-five, during a fasting spiritual retreat, he disappears into absolute silence.

He loves traveling, and singing, and beside India, lived for long periods in the Buddhist Southeast Asia: Japan, Thailand, Sri Lanka, Hong Kong, China and Tibet, to explore and study, out of curiosity and personal research, local cultures, both meeting people, and in the form of their rituals and religious practices applied to the life of every day.

Through the years, he studies and deepens different meditation techniques, for awakening consciousness, energy balancing, and personal evolution, which he practices and teaches. He leads meditation groups and sessions, conferences, retreats, and meetings in truth, in Italy, India, and the world, where he indicates the absolute.

Doctor of Metaphysical Science, Holistic Life Coach, Reiki Grand Master, Karuna Reiki®, Crystals, Shaman, and Meditation Master, he's the author of several books on spirituality and subjects dear to his heart. Married with Ma Advaita Krisana, he resides in the mainland of Venice, Italy. Write to Andrea Scarsi through his website at:

www.andrea-scarsi.com.

BOOKS BY ANDREA SCARSI

Answers For The Soul: Fragments of Eternal Wisdom
Blessings! Dedicated to Osho
Extraterrestrial Channeling: Alien Abduction Syndrome
Get Ready It's Happening: Surviving Gaia's Changes
Home Sweet Home Staging: Easy is Right
How To Ask A Woman Out: Gentlemen Only
Make Your Own Vineyard: Ex Vite Vita
O Iguana! My Iguana! Herbivore is Beautiful
Pearls of Wisdom: Tales of Ordinary Metaphysics
Reiki First Degree Manual
Reiki Second Degree Manual
Seeds Of Enlightenment: The Buddha Within
Tarot Reading Essentials: The New Basic Meaning Manual
The Art of Persuasion: How to Achieve Your Goals Ethically
The Art of Worrying: How to Enter and Exit it at Will
The Secret Of Meditation: The Inner Dimension
The Secret Of Metaphysical Science: Our Eternal Journey Through Infinite.

MANTRAS BY ANDREA SCARSI (SANDESH)

Mantras Maha Mantras di Sandesh & DJ Van Wood. CD.

A mantra is a Verbal Being acting as a bridge between the human and the divine. It carries our prayer, thankfulness, and gratitude. It is an entity in its own right and when we recite or sing it to communicate with the superior dimension, in addition to words and sound we also employ intention, energy, devotion and focus. All this raises us immediately. It raises our emotional state and makes us touch God.

A mantra is an introspective event turning to the multiple aspects of the One by evoking its symbolic names: Shiva, Brahma, Vishnu, Ganesha, Laxmi, Saraswati, Gurudev, Shanti; names representing the infinite manifestation of the cosmic cycle. They are magic formulas for amending the universal present, resolving the apparent fragmentation and recreating the union of consciousness with what is.

A mantra is to be recited and sung without interruption, to convey the intact message, and breathing comes between a recitation and the other. Let's get lost in the mantra, and let the vehicle, the human and the divine become one. This is the power of mantra. We recite it and go deeper and deeper, until melting what we were before, our intention, recitation, sound and collective energy, and manifesting unity once again, the yoga of consciousness, the absolute presence, whose supreme name is Om.

BOOKS BY ANDREA SCARSI IN ITALIAN

21 Giorni
A Proposito di Osho
Benedizioni!
Benvenuti ad Atlantide
Canalizzazioni Extraterrestri
Casa Dolce Casa Vendesi
Dhyana Yoga
Dispense Reiki Primo Livello
Dispense Reiki Secondo Livello
Dispense Reiki Terzo Livello Master
Il Maestro e l'Assassino
Il Segreto della Meditazione
Il Segreto della Scienza Metafisica
Il Silenzio dell'Assoluto
Immagina
La Cucina Vegetariana
L'Arte della Persuasione
L'Arte della Preoccupazione
L'Arte di Cambiare
L'Arte di Invitare una Donna
Le Compatibilità Zodiacali
Lettura dei Tarocchi
Massaggio Olistico
Notiziario Reiki
Perle di Saggezza
Risposte per l'Anima
Semi di Illuminazione
Transizione Vegetariana
Viaggio nel Mondo di Sotto
Zen Il Senso del Non Senso

Thank You for reading *Make Your Own Vineyard*.
I sincerely hope you find this book useful.
Dr. Andrea Scarsi (Sandesh)

Printed in Great Britain
by Amazon